GW00976075

EARLY MAN IN THE VALE OF YORK

York lies in the centre of Yorkshire at the junction of two rivers, the Foss and the Ouse, about 60km inland from the sea. At York the Ouse cuts through a moraine, sand and gravel left by retreating glaciers at the end of the last Ice Age. The moraine forms a ridge of high ground running east-west across the low-lying and in places marshy Vale of York. The ridge served as a natural causeway in prehistoric times and the river crossing point at York was, therefore, a focus for land- and water-based communications. Finds of stone and metal objects are evidence for human activity hereabouts over the last 6000 years.

Two thousand years ago the Ouse was wider than it is today and the average river level was as much as 3m lower. The Ouse was tidal until 1757 when Naburn lock was built downstream from York. Over the centuries the city's rivers have been forced into narrower channels and the course of the Foss has changed considerably due to alterations in the Norman and more recent periods.

Flint axes, c.3000 BC, found at Holgate Road

1

PREHISTORIC SETTLEMENT

There are many ancient and now invisible settlements in the immediate area. Excavations north of York near Easingwold, for example, revealed the remains of round huts of the 1st century BC surrounded by small fields defined by ditches. This is an Iron Age farmstead, where Celtic-speaking Britons once lived. Other research in the Vale of York seems to confirm that the Romans were greeted by a cleared and cultivated landscape with occasional woodland, scrub and marsh.

Iron Age cooking pot

on Age round huts near Easingwold, cut by modern plough marks and land drains

EBORACUM

In AD 71 the 5000 or so men of the ninth legion marched north from Lincoln. Their orders were to conquer the native tribe known as the Brigantes who occupied most of Britain between the Humber and the Scottish lowlands. For the legion's principal base in the region, the commander, Petilius Cerialis, chose a site on a spur of land between the Ouse and the Foss and established there a fortress which the Romans called *Eboracum*.

Intaglio of Fortuna

For the Romans York had many strategic advantages based on its good communications. The Ouse led to the Humber estuary and the North Sea, allowing supplies to be shipped in relatively easily. Land routes gave easy access to the valleys of the Pennines and North York Moors where British opponents might gather. York was favourably situated near to potentially rich agricultural land of the Vale of York and the nearby Wolds.

2

CONSTRUCTION METHODS AND MATERIALS

Excavation has demonstrated the use of a pre-determined plan in the fortress based on units of the Roman foot (0.296m). Within the playing-card shaped site of c.26 hectares (50 acres) there was a regular grid of streets. The lines of the two main thoroughfares, the *via praetoria* and *via principalis*, are closely followed today by Stonegate and Petergate respectively.

The earliest fortress buildings usually had a timber frame with the wall between the frame posts made of wattles (trimmed branches) coated with clay. The earliest defences consisted of a ditch in front of a rampart of clay and turf standing 3m high. There was a timber gate at the end of each of the main streets, and a palisade ran along the top of the rampart, with

look-out towers at regular intervals.

For later rebuilding work the Romans needed large quantities of building stone. Since there is none on the site of York itself, a massive operation using local waterways was used to bring it in. The

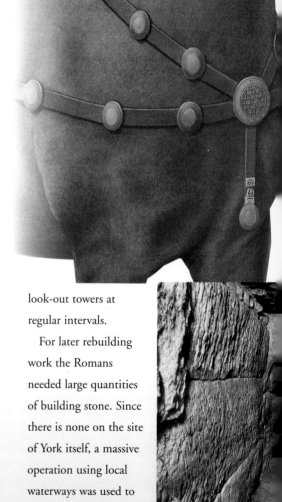

The sewer in the fortress ba

The archaeology of Roman York provides much information and detail about the military-based fortress complex and the civilian settlements which grew up around it. With the establishment of the fortress in the late 1st century came the alignment of the major streets, the *via principalis* and *via praetoria*, leading to roads outside the fortress which linked it to the forts in the region.

During the 2nd century there were rebuilding programmes in the fortress and on the defences. There is evidence for buildings being reconstructed in stone. Excavations within the fortress have revealed the headquarters (*principia*), barrack blocks and bath house with its great sewer. An impression of the 'grandeur that was Rome' can be gained in the York Minster Foundations where walls of the headquarters basilica can be seen, and there is part of a heated room from the baths in the Roman Bath public house. Other buildings in the fortress would have included a hospital, workshops and granaries, but no trace of them has yet been found. Extensive remains of the fortress defences still survive above and below ground. In the

Intaglio of Mars

's of Millstone Grit

principal stone types in Roman York include the fine-grained Magnesian Limestone from the Tadcaster area west of York. It was usually made into the small blocks which can, for example, be seen in the Multangular Tower. Jurassic oolite from the North York Moors is a more granular limestone which occurs in small, flat slabs.

There are also two types of sandstone. Millstone Grit is a coarse material which probably came from quarries in the Wetherby area close to the river Wharfe. It was used for massive load-bearing structures, and for coffins and tombstones. Elland Flag (now known as York Stone) came from the Bradford-Huddersfield area and was used for roofing and floors.

Stone walls were constructed using a high-quality lime mortar which, on occasions, is as hard as modern concrete and will challenge the most sophisticated modern breaking equipment.

EBORACUM

Museum Gardens, marking the west corner of the fortress, stands the Multangular Tower, one of the finest pieces of Roman military architecture in Europe. At the east corner, behind Aldwark, it is possible to see the fortress wall standing to its full original height.

The settlement which grew up south-east of the fortress in the late 1st and 2nd centuries was geared to providing services for the army. There was a grain warehouse at 39–41 Coney Street close to where ships would have pulled up on the banks of the Ouse. A jetty on the Foss has been found at Fossgate. Pottery and tile manufacture took place in the Peasholme Green area. In the later 2nd century this settlement was reorganised and the grain warehouse was replaced by a gravel street which ran along the river bank. Little else is known, although there was a bath house at the corner of High Ousegate and Spurriergate, and altars found in the Nessgate area suggest the presence of temples, one of which was dedicated to Hercules. There would also have been a large amphitheatre and it may have stood between St Andrewgate and St

ROMAN LIFE

Archaeology has told us a great deal about daily life in Roman York, especially about what its people ate and what they wore. Deposits of cereal grain, largely wheat, preserved by being charred in warehouse fires, show that the Romans ate lots of bread and porridge. Meat was usually beef, to judge by the huge quantity of cattle bones, although lamb, pork, fish and chicken were also consumed. Preserved pips and stones show that food items like figs, grapes and olives were imported from Mediterranean countries. Large pottery jars called amphorae brought olive oil from Spain and wine from Gaul (France).

Both men and women in Roman times dressed in a tunic tied or belted at the waist. Over this people wore a hooded cloak in cold and wet weather which was often fastened at the throat with a brooch. There were many different styles of shoes including slippers,

Face mas[k]

Bone hair pins

4

Saviourgate, where later Anglo-Scandinavian streets seem to have been laid out to avoid a large elliptical structure.

Settlement of the south-west bank of the Ouse probably began in the mid 2nd century. This area may have been deliberately kept clear of buildings in the late 1st and early 2nd centuries for military reasons. During the subsequent decades of the late 2nd century urban development appears to have been rapid and by the 3rd century there is evidence for expansion over the entire area defined by the medieval walls. These walls probably correspond to and overlie a pre-existing Roman defensive circuit. Evidence has been found for civic buildings including a market place, the administrative centre and public bath houses. There were temples to the gods Serapis and Mithras. A thriving commercial district probably included warehouses, workshops and riverside wharves. The fine houses of well-to-do residents stood on terraces overlooking the commercial centre and the river. They had amenities such as a piped water supply, private baths and underfloor heating, as well as mosaics and high-quality painted wall plaster.

Gold earrings

5

boots with nailed-on soles and others which were tied on with leather thongs. Roman women wore plenty of jewellery including rings, bracelets, earrings and necklaces. Men often had a seal ring which held a semi-precious gemstone, or intaglio carved with a distinctive design.

...tery flagon

A jar, a mortarium (mixing bowl), a flagon and a beaker

EBORACUM

The evidence clearly shows that by the 3rd century the main civilian settlement was prosperous. Its growth was probably based on servicing the needs of the army and acting as the region's market centre, redistributing agricultural products and manufactured goods (both made locally and brought in through the port from elsewhere in the Empire). When the Emperor Septimius Severus resided in York in 209–11 its civilian settlement had become the most important Roman town in northern Britain, although the population may not have exceeded 5000 people. Soon after Severus's death in York the town's importance was recognised when it became capital of the northern province of Roman Britain and was given the status of *colonia*, the highest that a Roman town could achieve.

Septimius Severus

By the middle of the 3rd century the Roman empire was suffering from civil war and barbarian attacks which affected its economic stability. In Roman York this is reflected by diminishing quantities of imported pottery and glass which suggest a decline in long-distance trade

The building at Wellington Row on fire

6

BURIALS

The Romans always buried their dead outside settlements, in accordance with Roman law, usually along the local main roads. At York cemetery sites have been found along the main approach roads from the south-west at Trentholme Drive, The Mount and Blossom Street, and from the south at Clementhorpe. Sites are known on the roads leading north-west in the Bootham area and south-east in the Fishergate area.

Burial in Roman times involved elaborate ceremonies and rituals which in the 1st and 2nd centuries accompanied cremation and burial of the ashes in pottery, glass or lead urns. By the end of the 2nd century cremation was no longer practised and the corpse was usually laid out in a 'bath-shaped' grave pit. Objects accompanied the dead as offerings to the gods or as symbolic gifts for the journey to the next world.

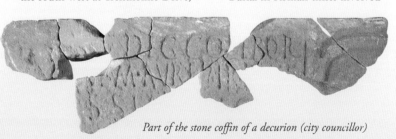

Part of the stone coffin of a decurion (city councillor)

Excavation of burnt timbers in a Roman building at Wellington Row

connections. After the restoration of order in the later 3rd century York remained the most important Roman centre in the north.

In the second half of the 4th century York underwent important changes prompted, in part, by the renewed political crises elsewhere in the Roman empire. By about 400 many men from York's garrison had been withdrawn to the Continent to fight in the civil wars. Those remaining at their posts probably kept their families in the old barrack blocks while other buildings became derelict and refuse accumulated around them. Recent research suggests that the so-called 'Anglian Tower', to be seen today near the Multangular Tower, was actually erected by the Romans, perhaps as part of a last attempt to strengthen the fortress defences. In the *colonia* archaeology has revealed that streets fell out of use, buildings were demolished and the remains were used as rubbish dumps by the last inhabitants of *Eboracum*.

Jet plaque fragment

7

Pottery vessels, which originally contained food and wine, are the most common grave offerings, but jewellery, caskets and many other items are also known. Many 4th century burials contain no grave goods and this may reflect the spread of Christianity which rejected pagan customs.

The wealthy erected grave monuments and York has a superb collection of tombstones. Their inscriptions and portraits give many insights into the life and times of the Roman population. On occasions, stone coffins were used for burials and some of these also bear inscriptions. At a site on Blossom Street excavations revealed the remains of a small mausoleum in which there had been at least three burials, perhaps from a single family.

Skeleton from a cemetery on Blossom Street

EOFORWIC

Anglian glass beads

The archaeological record is blank in the century or so after AD 400, leaving archaeologists to theorise about what impact the Roman military and political withdrawal had upon people living and working in York. We can take up the story again towards the end of the 5th century when we know that Germanic settlers from the coastal region of modern Germany and Denmark made their way to York. So-called Anglian occupation is represented by distinctive cremation cemeteries found at Heworth and on The Mount, which date to the later 5th/6th century.

From the writings of this period's great scholars, including the Venerable Bede and Alcuin of York, we know many historical facts about York. We are told that in 627 the Northumbrian King Edwin was converted to Christianity and was baptised in a newly built wooden church. This later became a cathedral and probably stood near the present Minster. In 735 York became an archbishopric, and a monastery was founded which became internationally renowned for its scholarship.

Cremation urns from The Mount and Heworth

8

THE CHURCH IN ANGLIAN YORK

In his grand plan for the conversion of Anglo-Saxon England in AD 601 Pope Gregory chose York to be the centre of Christianity in the North. The missionary Paulinus eventually reached the city a generation later, even though York itself may have been largely abandoned and in ruins. He baptised Edwin, King of Northumbria, in a small purpose-built wooden church which he dedicated to St Peter. Edwin's church was rebuilt in stone and but for the King's death in battle in AD 633–4 would have become the seat of an archbishopric. Paulinus fled and the bishops of Lindisfarne were probably responsible for the church at York until the episcopal see was restored in AD 664 following the Synod of Whitby.

Subsequently, York truly became the ecclesiastical capital of the North. Its bishop St Wilfrid began the first of a series of repairs and beautifications of the church which went on throughout the 8th century. Archaeology has so far revealed virtually nothing of the most important and impressive church in Northumbria. It is

Copper alloy and enamel brooch, c. Paragon Street

Eoforwic, as the settlement was now called, became a port of call for international merchants. The archaeological evidence for York's development through the Anglian period, however, is tantalisingly incomplete.

As yet, neither the Anglo-Saxon cathedral nor the monastery and its school have been discovered, though high quality sculpture of the period has been found under York Minster. The royal palace, if one existed, is equally elusive. Modern excavations throughout the old Roman fortress, *colonia* and suburbs have not revealed traces of the timber buildings which were normal at this period. In some places it is even difficult to distinguish any build-up of soil between late Roman deposits and 10th/11th century layers. Anglian

Cross-shaft, c.700–800, from York Minster; a Mediterranean design of a vine-scroll with birds

fortunate, therefore, that the writings of Bede and Alcuin give relatively full contemporary accounts.

These and other written sources show that by the end of the 8th century York was a town of churches — not only St Peter's and the monastery founded by Bishop Bosa, but such churches as Holy Wisdom, built for Archbishop Aethelberht in 778–80. A great library had grown up and no doubt a scriptorium to copy the books, as other ecclesiastical centres in England and on the Continent sought access to them. The Durham manuscript of Cassiodorus may be one of its products. The school at York attracted students from home and abroad; one of the most brilliant scholars was Alcuin, who after a long career at York was persuaded by the emperor Charlemagne to teach at the palace school at Aachen. There, and later at the monastery of St Martin at Tours, Alcuin was one of the main influences on the Carolingian renaissance. Through such contacts York had a formative role in the development of European culture in the 8th and 9th centuries.

objects are, however, found in small numbers on most excavated sites and suggest widespread occupation or activity, at a relatively low density, throughout the former Roman town and fortress. There is increasing evidence, mainly from pieces of imported pottery, that the river banks were again a focus of trade. Activity was taking place in a number of discrete areas, particularly along the banks of the Ouse. In the Coppergate/Castlegate area there may have been a major Anglian church on the site of St Mary Castlegate. Nearby, the dramatic discovery of the Coppergate Anglian helmet was made, yet no Anglian structures were found at the Coppergate excavations. In 1985–6, however, important settlement remains of the 8th–9th century came to light at Fishergate, 1km downstream from the old Roman fortress, below the confluence of the rivers Foss and Ouse. Traces of several rectangular timber buildings were recovered, with associated ditches, rubbish pits, wells and latrines. A broad range of craft and industrial activity was represented. Iron and other metals, glass, bone and antler, wood and leather were some of the raw materials employed, and textile making also took place. The site may be an example of the

10

ANGLIAN ART IN YORK

The abstract interlace patterns of Anglian art survive only on metal, stone and bone objects — lost are the rich textiles, leather and other items hinted at by the magnificent illuminated manuscripts which still exist. The stylised interlaced animal patterns of the Anglo-Saxon homelands continued to evolve in England, eventually acquiring

naturalistic elements (Christian symbols, vine-scroll) with the influence of papal missions from the Mediterranean during the early 7th century. A good example of animal interlace can be seen on a bone handle from Fishergate and an extremely stylised beast's head adorns a silver strap-end from Rougier Street.

The spectacular helmet found by construction workers laying the foundations for the Jorvik Viking Centre dates to about 750–75 and is made of iron with brass decoration. Already old and mended when buried, the helmet bears the inscription '*In the name of our Lord Jesus Christ, the Holy Spirit (and) God; and to all we say Amen. Oshere*'. It is an apt testimony to the

Silver strap-end, Rougier Street

The Cop, c.750–7

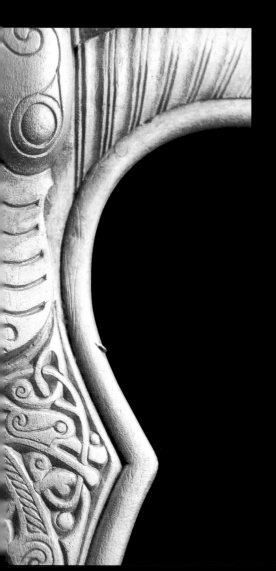

trading centres, known as wics, which began to develop in late 7th or early 8th century England, often close to old Roman centres. Similar sites have been found at London, Southampton and Ipswich. It remains to be seen if the Fishergate site is on the edge or in the middle of a much larger Anglian settlement which extends along the rivers.

8th century silver coins

11

achievements of skilled craftsmen working in the artistic and scholarly Northumbrian world of which Alcuin and York were so much a part.

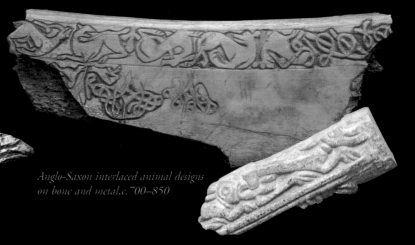

*Anglo-Saxon interlaced animal designs
on bone and metal.c.700–850*

net,

JORVIK

The port of *Eoforwic*, perhaps serving the needs of the Northumbrian kings and archbishops, would have been well known to 8th century seafarers, and it is surprising that it was untroubled by early Viking raids which had plagued much of the country. However, in 866 the Northumbrian kingdom was racked by political unrest and, taking advantage of this, the 'great pagan army' seized *Eoforwic*. Within a decade a new Scandinavian kingdom based at *Jorvik* had been established. By the time the last Viking king Eric Bloodaxe was expelled from *Jorvik* in 954, the intermarriage of 'locals' and Vikings had created an Anglo-Scandinavian culture which survived until the Norman Conquest. The impact of this takeover is still apparent in the York street names incorporating the old Norse word *gata* which means street, whilst below ground physical remains of *Jorvik* survive.

With the arrival of the Vikings, the Anglian settlement at Fishergate was abandoned and a new commercial heart grew up along streets leading down to a new river crossing at Ouse Bridge, on previously deserted

EVERYDAY LIFE

The evidence from Coppergate paints an image of squalid and filthy living conditions in the Viking settlement. Rubbish had to be disposed of in backyards; discarded building materials of thatch, wattle and timber, food and butchery remains, industrial debris and human waste were all deposited in the confines of the closely spaced tenements. As a result the ground level was rising by up to 1cm a year in this part of York. This rapid build-up, in combination with the natural drainage pattern, produced the moist anaerobic conditions which prevented the decay of organic material. Not only are plants and insects from the natural environment preserved but also items in everyday use like wooden cups and buckets, bone knife handles and hair combs, and more personal items like leather shoes, a woollen sock and a girl's silk head-dress.

land closer to the old Roman defences. Part of this area was explored in 1976–81 at Coppergate, now the site of the Jorvik Viking Centre, where extensive excavations have provided an insight into the nature of the settlement. Thatched single-storey timber buildings were laid out along a street; each stood within a long narrow plot running down to the river Foss, and was separated from its neighbours by wattle fences. By about 975 these buildings had been replaced by ones with plank-built semi-basements, standing in two ranks along the street. Debris found in and around these buildings shows that they were both homes and workshops for specialised industries.

Metalworking took place at several properties, producing everyday items like knives, keys and cheap jewellery. Manufacture of the standard tableware of the period, wooden cups and bowls, gave Coppergate its name — 'street of the cup-makers'. Small items of jewellery like beads and rings were made from amber and jet, whilst bone and antler were used both for professionally made articles like combs, and for home-made ice skates. Pottery was mass-produced, textiles and leather goods made, and

13

Coppergate buildings in c.950 (above) and c.975 (left)

Wooden panpipes, lyre bridge and bone whistle

Blacksmiths' products

JORVIK

there is evidence for glass working. The great majority of raw materials came from the city's hinterland, which also provided the dietary mainstays of beef, mutton, pork and fish, cereals for baking and brewing, and by-products including leather, horn and wool. Goods from Scotland, Ireland, the Rhineland, Holland and Scandinavia reached York, and from the East came silks and, perhaps, perfumes, oils and spices.

Silver brooch

Smaller scale excavations across the River Ouse on Micklegate — the '*great street*' leading to the river crossing — dramatically show the change from Roman to Viking Age layout; a 10th century semi-basement building was cut diagonally into the top of a massive buried Roman wall. Nearby, on the river-front in Skeldergate, there were also signs of a new layout. Some areas, however, remain largely unknown and amongst them the former Roman fortress stands out as a place where Anglo-Scandinavian occupation is virtually unrecognised.

14

VIKING AGE COINS, POLITICS AND PROPAGANDA

By 900 the Vikings upgraded Northumbria's silver coinage, minting pennies of the quality common to the rest of England. In the absence of a detailed, contemporary written account, these coins are important to understanding the history of *Jorvik*. For example, they show that by about 905 the Viking rulers were flaunting alliance with the church.

Some coins have religious mottoes, proclaiming (in abbreviated Latin) '*The Lord God Almighty is King*'. Others are dedicated to St Peter, patron of York's cathedral. The Anglo-Scandinavian mixture of Christianity and Viking myth is

Silver pennies ar an iron coin die

shown in the hammer symbol of the Germanic god Thor which appears on some of these St Peter coins. When the English king Athelstan captured the city in 927 his new

The influence of Christianity is apparent in the foundation of many of the city's churches during the 10th century, by which time the entire population seems to have been at least nominally Christian. Building a church not only ensured one's spiritual future (as lavish pagan burial goods had done in the past) but also brought income from church fees. The Scandinavian newcomers seem soon to have adopted the funerary customs of the natives, although two graves found close to the church of St Mary Bishophill Junior contained individuals buried in the early 10th century with distinctly Scandinavian goods. Stone grave-markers decorated with interlace patterns, stylised animals and figures became fashionable at this time and are found at several York churches.

Jorvik had become an affluent centre of manufacture and commerce, eyed covetously by English and Viking kings alike, and not surprisingly the city's defences were modernised. The walls on the north-east and north-west sides of the Roman fortress were built up with earthen ramparts topped by a wooden palisade. They were probably extended to the two rivers on the lines later

15

A scene in Jorvik Viking Centre

York coins boasted that he was '*Rex To. Brit.*' (King of all Britain). But his successor, the Viking Olaf Sigtryggson, proclaimed his militant independence by coins which, uniquely, carried his title in the Old Norse language, ONLAF CUNUNC, coupled with a representation of a bird, perhaps Odin's raven. His successor, the less capable Sigtryg Sigtryggson,

attempted to bolster support with a warlike sword and banner design.

The last Viking king of York, Erik Bloodaxe, also used a Viking sword design; it was never used again after his dethronement and death in 954, and York's later coins all followed the standard English pattern.

Fragmentary stone grave-marker

JORVIK

followed by the 13th century stone walls, although the other sides of the fortress seem to have been abandoned, perhaps to allow access to the river. Across the Ouse the Roman town walls may have been rebuilt. There may also have been a small defended enclosure on the south-east side of the Foss, but the line of the later medieval stone wall in Walmgate was certainly not defended at this time.

In time of attack these ramparts could protect not only the townsfolk but also frightened country dwellers. There were other, smaller defensible areas in and around the city, where the elite lived, and it is likely that the Viking kings had a palace. Although it has never been found, it may have been just outside the old Roman gateway in the area now called King's Square,

Brooch from the Low Countries

16

Amber from the Baltic

YORK AND THE VIKING WORLD

The Viking capture of York and settlement in Yorkshire was part of a major expansion of Scandinavian influence in the 9th and 10th centuries. In pursuit of their differing interests, Scandinavian warriors, traders and petty kings all sought advantage in new lands. Their skills in shipbuilding and navigation brought distant shores within easier reach; coast-hopping took them east along the Baltic Sea and up the Russian rivers, and down familiar routes to the rich settlements of the Low Countries and France where, ultimately, they settled in Normandy. The Vikings were active too in most parts of the British Isles; in addition to northern and eastern England, the Northern and Western Isles of Scotland were settled, and in Ireland a series of bases were established including Dublin, Waterford, Cork and Limerick which developed into important trading centres. Venturing further out into the Atlantic, Vikings discovered the Faroe Islands and Iceland, stepping stones to later exploration and colonisation of Greenland and North America.

Soapstone bowl fragment from Shetland

Conungsgurtha ('King's Court') as it became known. Later, when the city was controlled by Anglo-Scandinavian earls on behalf of the English kings, there is evidence that they lived on the north-west side of the fortress. The present St Olave's church in Marygate is successor to the one in which Earl Siward was buried in 1055, within what was described as *Earlsburh*, 'the earl's residence'.

17

Norwegian whetstone

Cowrie shell from the Red Sea

Lead customs' receipt

Irish ringed pins

NORMAN YORK

York's continuing political and economic importance is recorded by the events of 1066. The invading Norwegian king Harald Hardraada fought and won the first battle of his campaign for England at Fulford, now a York suburb. Five days later the English King Harold, hot-foot from the south, defeated the Norwegians at nearby Stamford Bridge. Racing south again, he in turn was beaten at Hastings by Duke William of Normandy, thus changing the course of English history.

For nearly two years York saw nothing of the conquerors, but in 1068 William marched north. The city surrendered, and William marked his claim by building a castle. Early in 1069 an English rebellion had some success at York before William returned northwards to stifle it. He plundered York, and tightened his grip by building a second castle, opposite the first, at the downstream limit of the city's defences. It may have been intended to block river-borne attacks on the city by stretching a chain between the castles.

In autumn 1069 a joint Anglo-Danish uprising and invasion again made York a target. The Norman garrison set fire to timber buildings around the castles, to deprive the

THE BATTLE OF FULFORD

It is rare to find archaeological remains linking individuals to an historical event. However, the excavation of a mid 11th century cemetery at St Andrew's, Fishergate, revealed some surprising evidence. Among the men, women and children of the parochial churchyard was a group of young adult men, lying in rows, who may all have been buried at the same time. All displayed unhealed wounds sustained as the result of a fierce battle. Whilst it is not possible to be certain when these fatal wounds were sustained, this cemetery was close to the site of the Battle of Fulford.

Skull with sword cuts

Arrowhead

Whalebone sword pommel

rebels of useful siege materials; this reportedly became a widespread blaze and destroyed much of the city, although no trace of the fire has been seen in any excavation. Yet when they ventured out of their strongholds, the Normans were defeated by the newly arrived Danes, who destroyed the castles. The Danes, however, retreated when William approached York, and the king spent Christmas 1069 in the city and rebuilt his two castles.

One of these eventually became known as York Castle. Its typical motte, or defensive mound, still stands with the 13th century Clifford's Tower on top. It was additionally strengthened by the artificial lake 'The King's Fishpond', formed by damming the River Foss. Its sister motte, across the river, is now known as Baile Hill. There the motte had been built up of layers of soil and a large central rectangular timber structure, possibly a tower, was erected on the summit later in the Norman period. At Clifford's Tower also the mound was built up in layers. Extensive traces of burnt timber found below the present summit may be evidence of the burning in 1190, when the castle was sacked in an anti-Jewish riot.

19

Castle ditch excavated at Tower Street; motte and Clifford's Tower in background

12th century leather knife-scabbard

NORMAN YORK

Documentary and architectural evidence show how the Church flourished under Norman stimulus. The Anglo-Scandinavian cathedral was destroyed by fire in 1069. It was replaced on a new site, nearby, in a new, Norman, style and on a new east-west alignment. Excavations below York Minster have revealed the remarkable timber and mortar raft foundation laid by the Norman builders to support their cathedral. They built an aisleless structure, regularly buttressed, with a central tower, transepts, and an apse at the east end, altogether about two-thirds the length of the present cathedral. Parts can still be seen below the Minster.

Elsewhere we have evidence for new parish churches and the founding of new religious houses such as St Mary's Abbey, which became the richest and most influential Benedictine monastery in northern England. Close by, but within the city walls, St Leonard's Hospital was built. It housed several hundred sick and infirm, as well as providing food and care for out-

ST WILLIAM OF YORK

Of the six canonised bishops and archbishops of York, only St William was buried here. Born into a powerful family — his father Henry I's chancellor, his mother a grand-daughter of William the Conqueror — William was appointed Archbishop of York in 1141. Disgraced and removed from office in 1148, he successfully visited Rome to plead for

reinstatement. Returning to York in 1154 a large crowd joined him as he crossed the timber Ouse bridge, which promptly collapsed hurling citizens into the river. Weeping, William made the sign of the cross over the calamity and all were saved. William, however, was dead within a month (allegedly poisoned at Mass). His sanctity was indicated by a subsequent spate of miracles.

In 1223 sweet smelling oil flowed from his tomb, still to be seen in the Minster. With the expediency of a cathedral lacking a saint, William was canonised in 1227 and a shrine erected. In the medieval world pilgrimage to shrines was commonplace and a lucrative source of income for the church. Cheap souvenirs were locally produced and pedalled to pilgrims. Two of these,

Am
St V
shri

patients. Remains of both monastery and hospital survive to this day. Examples of fine Norman doorways can be seen at St Denys Walmgate and St Margaret Walmgate.

Apart from churches, visible evidence for buildings of the Norman period is scarce. Traces of only two Norman houses, both of stone, survive above ground; one is encased within the Treasurer's House near York Minster and the other stands off Stonegate. Originally there were probably many more, for the foundations of several others have been excavated, in Skeldergate and Aldwark, and below the Merchant Adventurers' Hall.

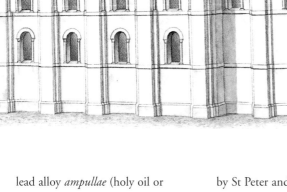

Norman doorway from St Denys church

21

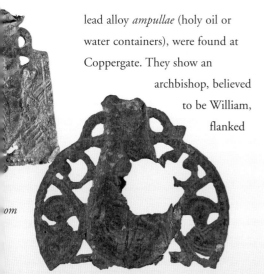

lead alloy *ampullae* (holy oil or water containers), were found at Coppergate. They show an archbishop, believed to be William, flanked by St Peter and St Paul.

St William does not seem to have had a great following, and his shrine had fallen from use before the Privy Council's order to demolish shrines in 1541. Some has, however, survived within the fabric of other buildings in the city. Fragments were built into houses at Precentor's Court, some were found in a garden near Clifford's Tower,

and most recently a fragment of a niche came to light in excavations at The Bedern. Enough pieces are now in the Yorkshire Museum to give a good impression of how the shrine must have looked.

NORMAN YORK

Jet gaming pieces

Outside the defences, suburbs may also have been developing in the later Norman period. Most of them were probably no more than a line of houses along either side of the main approach roads, extending only a short way outside the gates. To the north-east, however, the name Newbiggin, which is first recorded in the late 12th century, may refer to a new, deliberately planned suburb with main streets including Groves Lane, Monkgate and Love Lane.

Norman documents make it clear that York's military, political, religious and economic importance for the north of England was so great that within a few generations of the Norman Conquest the city was apparently thriving once more. Streets and open spaces served as markets; tolls were collected on incoming goods as they entered the city gates. York also continued to be a major port, and c.1125 there is a reference to the presence of boats from Ireland and Germany. By 1130 prosperous and influential townspeople had formed themselves into a trading guild with its own meeting house. Attempts by

22

Bootham Bar; the central arch is Norman

citizens to rid themselves of interference from the King's county sheriff finally met success in 1213 when they bought the rights to self-government.

Some areas remained outside the citizens' control. The castle stayed in royal hands. The Archbishop had the cathedral precincts, later including the College of Vicars Choral at Bedern, as well as rights over part of the city in the Walmgate-Fishergate areas and Baile Hill. Other religious houses and institutions, such as St Leonard's Hospital, claimed independent rights which brought financial benefits. They also enforced their own justice; St Mary's Abbey, for example, had its gallows at Garrow Hill, south-east of the city.

Walrus ivory seal of Snarrus the toll-collector

Archaeological recording of the walls often reveals a complex sequence of rebuildings

23

THE CITY WALLS

The Normans had taken over a city defended with ditches outside earth ramparts capped with timber palisades. Their first contribution was to rebuild some of the gateways in stone, and two of these can still be seen at Bootham Bar and Micklegate Bar. In the 12th century they made the last addition to the defended area when the Walmgate suburb was enclosed.

During the Norman period there was haphazard removal of surviving parts of the Roman fortress walls which no longer marked the city's limit. In places along the south-west frontage by the River Ouse, and up the south-east side by St Andrewgate and Jubbergate, even the foundation stones were dug out for re-use elsewhere. Stone walls replacing the timber palisades were built from c.1250 onwards and strengthened occasionally up until 1745.

City walls at Fishergate-Walmgate

MEDIEVAL YORK

From the 13th century onwards documents survive in increasing numbers, but they are mostly concerned with important religious or secular institutions or with the wealthier citizens, and deal with only some aspects of medieval life. In general, they show that York continued to be a leading provincial town until about 1475. Its prosperity was based upon its roles as the main administrative and judicial centre for northern England for both church and state. Supplying the needs of these institutions, and of visitors who came to York because of them, was a key reason for York's wealth. Equally important was a continuation of the city's trade, not only within its immediate hinterland, but throughout England and overseas.

York's location, 325km north of London, made it a good base for military campaigns against the Scots. Its size and wealth also meant that it was a useful political balance to London. For these reasons, many English monarchs came to York. Henry III left his mark by ordering that York Castle should be rebuilt in stone c.1250; his work

24

GUILD HALLS

York has four surviving guild halls: the Guild Hall, behind the Mansion House in St Helen's Square, built by the city and the Guild of Saints Christopher and George (c.1449–59); the Merchant Taylors' Hall, Aldwark, founded by a religious guild which developed into a merchants' company in the 15th century; St Anthony's Hall, Peasholme Green, built by the guild of the same name (c.1450); and the Merchant Adventurers' Hall, Fossgate (c.1357).

The Merchant Adventurers' Hall, as it is now called, is one of York's most exceptional medieval buildings. It was originally built to house the communal meeting hall, chapel and undercroft hospital of the Fraternity of the Holy Trinity, a medieval social, religious and charitable mutual association. The guild comprised two separate operations, a secular business side and a fraternity which undertook religious affairs. This was typical during the period when the role of the merchant was regarded as little better than usury, an un-Christian act, and, therefore using profits for religious devotion and good works was seen as justification for the

included the four-lobed keep called Clifford's Tower, which stands on top of the earthen motte.

Henry III's command may have encouraged the citizens to rebuild the town's defences in stone. This work seems to have started in about 1250, although it was over a hundred years before the entire wooden palisade was replaced. The citizens took this opportunity to block a Norman gateway on the site of the Roman fortress north-east gate, which was approached through the cathedral precinct and thus controlled by the archbishop. Instead they built what survives as Monk Bar; this required a change to the street layout inside the walls, with part of Goodramgate closed and its line diverted abruptly to the new gate.

Trade was always more important than manufacturing as a source of wealth, and York's medieval merchants relied heavily on traffic along the River Ouse. Throughout the Middle Ages steps were taken to ensure adequate docking and storage facilities. The river's edge was reclaimed by dumping rubbish inside revetments of

The Merchant Adventurers' Hall and attached chapel as it may have looked c.1375

business activity. Hospitals became commonly associated with guild halls, but they functioned as almshouses rather than as infirmaries.

Over the years the building has been extended, notably with a two-storey Elizabethan annexe towards Fossgate. As ground level outside has been raised, probably to counteract flooding from the nearby River Foss, so too has the undercroft's floor. Excavation in 1995 showed it was originally 0.6m lower, and revealed well-preserved traces of internal partitions which subdivided the hospital into separate cubicles. It was also discovered that a Norman stone house stood on the site. It had been partially demolished so that about 1.7m of its walls survived. At least part of the 14th century Hall had then been deliberately built upon the Norman walls, using them as a strong foundation.

14th century gold brooch, inscribed IHESUS NAZ, *from the Merchant Adventurers' Hall*

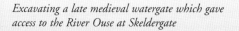

Excavating a late medieval watergate which gave access to the River Ouse at Skeldergate

25

MEDIEVAL YORK

timber or stone which were built out into the water. Excavation has shown that this was done by people on their own properties, and that quite elaborate wharves or staithes, slipways and watergates were created. Although by 1350 Hull overtook York in importance as a port and came to dominate cross-channel trade, York's waterfronts remained busy, as goods were trans-shipped to and from Hull, or brought to York along the rivers which flow into the Ouse or the Humber. Magnificent guild halls were built by the city's merchants.

The most important local exports were grain, wool and later the cloth for which Yorkshire became famous. The major overseas markets were the Low Countries, Germany, France and the Baltic. Foreign imports included wine, first from France and later from Germany and Portugal. Most of the other imported goods were also raw materials or foodstuffs which leave no archaeological trace. The visible evidence for this trade consists of pottery vessels, including French jugs, German cups and mugs, and Dutch cooking vessels.

26

MEDIEVAL PASTIMES

Archaeology provides evidence for the lighter side of life in the medieval period. Board games were popular, judging by the number of gaming or playing pieces found. They are usually made of bone; most are simple discs, but sometimes more elaborate pieces are made from jet. Dice indicate that not only skill but also chance played its part in these pastimes. A rare discovery shows that a game like bowls was played in York; the wooden bowl was made from ash.

Music making included the simplest of instruments, such as whistles made from the leg bones of geese found at Coppergate, and the more complex such as the harp, as shown by the discovery of bone pegs, which tightened the strings, from the site of the Vicars Choral College at Bedern.

A set of eight waxed tablets, excavated in Swinegate, brings us in direct contact with the life of one medieval person. Match-box sized, they measure just 30 x 50mm, and were kept together in a decorated

*Swinegate
modern rec*

York continued in its role as a focus for craftwork and manufacture. This was carried out by what were presumably family businesses, although success and expansion increasingly led to the employment of additional workers. Some craft guilds, such as the leatherworkers, existed before 1200, providing a mix of professional, social and charitable benefits for their members. Documents list the wide variety of crafts which were practised; archaeology can explore their workshop setting, their technologies, as revealed in manufacturing debris, and their finished products.

York supplied a large area with church fixtures and fittings, and several different aspects of this trade have been explored in excavation. Traces of glass window manufacture have been found off Stonegate, where St Helen's was the glaziers' guild church. In Bedern a bronze foundry which operated c.1250–1500 has been discovered, which included bells as well as cauldrons in its range of products. Hornpot Lane, not surprisingly, was where horners worked, flattening out cow or goat horn to make window panes and lanterns as well as drinking horns, spoons and many other items.

27

A richer merchant's house as it might have looked c.1500

ts: a
on
leather cover. They are both the smallest and the finest set to survive from Europe, where only about 150 sets are known. Although once common, such tablets were both fragile and likely to decay when thrown away. In this case, painstaking conservation allowed the tablets, which had stuck together, to be separated, and their secrets to be revealed.

Scribed into the wax c.1350 are jottings on three very different topics which still strike a chord today. One, in Latin, is a draft for a legal document of some sort; another seems to be a set of accounts, although its details are unclear. But it is not all business; the third is more personal — a poem with a love interest, written in Middle English, and including the repeated line '*She said to me nothing not no*' which may be updated as '*She didn't say yes, but she didn't say no*'.

MEDIEVAL YORK

Documents suggest that investing in property was an important source of income for York's well-to-do medieval citizens. Yet although York has many timber-framed buildings which have a distinctly 'medieval' appearance, many are relatively late in date, from the 15th–17th centuries. Apart from the remains of Norman stone houses, there are no 12th or 13th century domestic buildings to be seen in York. The earliest accurately dated one to survive is the two-storey terrace called Our Lady's Row in Goodramgate, dated by documents to 1316. Archaeology, however, has uncovered traces of 12th and 13th century timber buildings and can also fill in gaps in knowledge about later medieval structures.

The archaeological evidence for such buildings comes mainly from their foundations and footings. It shows a progression in building techniques from the Norman period, when foundations consisted of either horizontal or vertical timbers, in direct contact with the earth, to

Stone foundations like these, in Swinegate

28

WELLS AND CESS-PITS

The homes and workshops forming the commercial core of medieval York didn't have lawns and flowerbeds around them; instead they were surrounded by a strictly utilitarian environment notable for rubbish, cess-pits and wells.

Families had to get rid of their own rubbish, and the easiest option was disposal in their backyards. Sometimes it was strewn or heaped up on the surface; alternatively, it was buried in pits. Some were dug originally as cess-pits, and biological analysis of the cess deposits provides vital information about topics such as diet and health. Eventually, a cess-pit was usually

backfilled with normal domestic rubbish and soil, and another dug nearby.

Deeper pits were dug to act as wells. Their shafts were lined with casks, with a wooden framework, or with stone or brick, which served to support the sides and act as a simple filter. The

13th/14th century and later structures when the main timbers rested on pad stones or dwarf walls to protect them from the danger of rotting. Another contemporary change was in roofing material, with thatch being replaced by tiles. This made a considerable difference to the appearance of individual buildings and to the whole townscape, and was an improvement in weather-proofing and, perhaps, in maintenance costs, as well as reducing fire risk.

Decorative bronze fitting from The Bedern

Together, these changes led to less frequent repair and rebuilding, and so helped to cut down the amount of organic building debris lying around. Without this organic sponge to soak up water, less moisture was kept in the soil, and the whole process resulted in drier, more pleasant living and working conditions. All of this was of additional benefit because in the 13th century the previously open yards to the rear of each tenement plot were increasingly built upon – another sign of York's growing prosperity and

29

supported timber-framed 14th–15th century buildings such as Barley Hall, off Stonegate

ground water which filled the wells had passed through quite foul conditions, however, and

was not fit for drinking unless heated in the production of ale or beer.

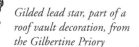

Gilded lead star, part of a roof vault decoration, from the Gilbertine Priory

population. Even the great plague, the so-called Black Death of 1349, had no long-term impact on the size of York's population; the city continued to act as a mecca for country folk hoping to improve their living standards.

Throughout all this period, as architectural fashions changed, the cathedral church was gradually altered and enlarged, so that at last nothing obvious remained above ground from the Norman church. The rebuilding required huge amounts of money, materials and labour, and the skills of stonemasons, woodcarvers, glass painters and leadworkers. By 1472 the Minster more or less as we know it today had been completed, and a great service of dedication was held in that year.

The monasteries and other religious houses, and the parish churches, were also altered or rebuilt as circumstances, fashion and finances dictated. For example, excavation has shown that the Gilbertine Priory in Fishergate was largely modernised in the mid 14th century; this was probably because its patron, the Bishop of

30

CHURCHES, MONASTERIES, COLLEGES AND HOSPITALS

By the end of the Middle Ages York must have seemed a city full of churches. Physically dominated by the Minster and the great Benedictine abbey of St Mary, it had no less than eight monasteries and friaries, over 40 parish churches, innumerable chapels and chantries, two major ecclesiastical colleges and no less than 31 hospitals or maisons dieu. Within

the city walls a substantial area was taken up by the cathedral precinct or by the monasteries and their precincts. Each main order clearly wanted a presence close to the heart of ecclesiastical matters in the North. With a parish church every 200 metres, even Ouse Bridge had its chapel of St William.

The great ecclesiastical corporations also owned much of

the rest of the city; many of the domestic properties in Stonegate, for example, belonged to York Minster. Further properties were owned by the monasteries, some from far afield, which needed somewhere for their monks to live when visiting the city.

Recently, archaeologists have

Lincoln, was also Chancellor of England and wanted a suitably up-to-date York residence. In the College of Vicars Choral at The Bedern there was a move away from communal living for the 36 priests towards individual privacy within what were separate rooms, divided off within the earlier open-plan buildings. And the surviving parish churches all include a variety of architectural styles, the result of individual donors paying for a particular part of the building — an aisle, a chapel, the chancel — to be rebuilt. This process has also been investigated in excavations; periodic enlargements of a church often result in ever bigger foundations, one around the other, like a set of Russian dolls.

Gilbertine Priory Church, c.1300–1350; only foundations and graves survived the dissolution in 1538

31

made determined efforts to excavate at least a sample of these properties as their sites have been redeveloped. The Gilbertine Priory of St Andrew was traced from its origins in 1202 to its demolition in the 16th century and Clementhorpe Nunnery has been partly excavated.

The small parish churches of St Helen-on-the-Walls in Aldwark and All Saints in Peasholme Green have been traced from origins to post-medieval demolition. Almost the whole of the College of the Vicars Choral of York Minster has been excavated, revealing its story from about 1250 through extensive development in the 14th century to post-medieval times. Both the

hospitals of St Nicholas in Hull Road and St Mary in the Horsefair beneath the present Union Terrace Car Park have also been excavated.

Parchment prickers, part of a scribe's equipment, are found on monastic and religious sites

MEDIEVAL YORK

In the century between c.1450 and c.1550 York's wealth declined and its population shrank, while newer manufacturing and trading towns such as Wakefield, Hull and Leeds took away its business. As decline struck home there was no demand for any major new buildings after c.1450, and even the upkeep of some existing parish churches proved a difficult burden. Royal policy brought great changes to the city when, in 1536–9, Henry VIII suppressed the monasteries and friaries. In York this affected Benedictine monks and nuns, Augustinian canons, Carmelite monks, both Dominican and Franciscan friars, and Gilbertine monks; their churches and precincts were confiscated and sold. Virtually all the buildings were torn down for their scrap value; glorious architecture was burnt in lime-kilns in order to convert stonework into lime-mortar. Only parts of St Mary's Abbey and Holy Trinity Priory remain; the other sites were eventually redeveloped.

The city corporation seized an opportunity and decided in 1547 to shut several parish churches, saying they were surplus to requirements. By 1586, 15 parishes had been amalgamated with others and their churches

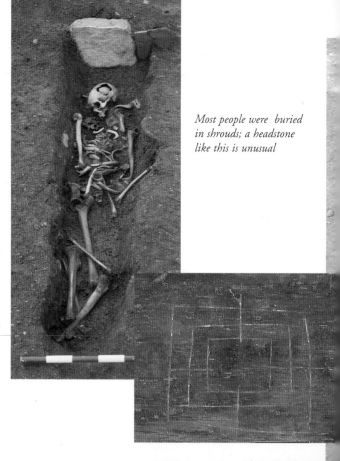

Most people were buried in shrouds; a headstone like this is unusual

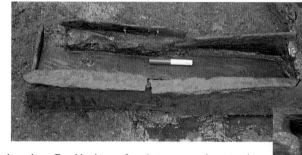

Medieval wooden coffins, like this one from Swinegate, rarely survive; here the lid has a gaming board marked out on it!

MEDIEVAL PEOPLE

The churchyards of York were often larger in medieval times than they are today, and redevelopment often brings us face-to-face with the people of earlier eras. Study of the cemetery populations from St Helen-on-the-Walls and St Andrew, Fishergate, has contributed greatly to our knowledge, shedding light on topics such as health, diet, appearance and life expectancy.

Medieval people looked much like people do today, although they were a few centimetres shorter on average. What distinguished the medieval population from today's was the higher mortality rate for infants, children and, due to the complications of childbirth, women under the age of 35. Even if they survived these potentially lethal hazards, adults rarely lived much beyond 50. Many diseases and injuries can be detected by study of the pathology of the bones. Poor diet could lead to the curved bones typical of rickets, and there was much joint disease.

There is also archaeological evidence of the medieval Jewish

closed; most of the buildings had already been demolished, and only St Andrew's in St Andrewgate survives today. The other sites, including their graveyards, were sold on, and put to other uses.

The Reformation of religious practices also saw the closure of all the city's chantry chapels, where prayers were said for their benefactors, as well as some colleges, chapels, guilds and hospitals. The property owned by these institutions, which had provided them with income, was also confiscated and sold. Overall, there was a revolution in property ownership and in the appearance of York; within a lifetime, many long-established and substantial religious buildings disappeared.

Some, however, could be adapted to a new use. A classic case was St Mary's Hospital in the Horsefair, at Union Terrace. This was originally built in the early 13th century as a Carmelite Friary, but within a century it became a hospital when the friars moved to another site. In 1557 it was taken over by St Peter's School, which stayed there until the Civil War.

Lime-kiln built by the demolition men at the Gilbertine Priory

community which flourished between 1220 and 1260, before royal taxation crippled its businesses and ultimately it was expelled from England in 1290.

The synagogue in Coney Street has not been found but at Jewbury, just outside the city walls, the Jewish burial ground was discovered, and partly excavated in advance of a major redevelopment. Some 500 skeletons were recovered and recorded, giving a unique insight into the burial practices of English medieval Jews. In sharp contrast to contemporary medieval Christian cemeteries, the burial ground was regularly laid out and carefully maintained. The skeletons are reburied in gardens alongside the Jewbury car park.

TUDOR AND STUART YORK

After its century or so of decline, York was increasingly revitalised from 1539 when it became the seat of the King's Council in the Northern Parts. This body governed northern England on the King's behalf until 1641, during the Civil War. Housed at King's Manor, within the old St Mary's Abbey complex, it made York a secular and judicial centre, in parallel with the church courts and administration, and brought all sorts of business to the city. The knock-on effects included, for example, a steady trade in the supply of parchment, made from sheepskin, which was used for keeping records. Lodging houses and inns flourished, and commerce improved too, with the city's merchants re-organising themselves into the Company of Merchant Adventurers. There was a considerable amount of new building, mostly domestic, during the second half of the 16th century and the first half of the 17th century. New buildings included magnificent town houses for the aristocracy, although none remain today. When the thrones of Scotland and England were united in the person of King James I in 1603, it even seemed possible that York would become the joint nation's new, centrally placed capital, but the idea collapsed.

St Mary's Tower; note the irreg...

One of the earliest plans of York, in c.1618

THE ARCHAEOLOGY OF BRICKS

With the exception of the stone-built churches and religious houses, late medieval York was city of timber-framed buildings. From the 14th century onwards, however, a new, highly durable and, in due course, cheap material was beginning to appear which by the mid 17th century would be used for housing of all grades. This was brick, first used in a major building in 1357–61 for the Merchant Adventurers' Hall, although excavations show that at this time it was usually used for the footings of timber buildings and for cess-pit linings. Early bricks are of irregular shape and only about 2 inches thick, but size gradually increased and quality improved. Brick rather than stone was used for the so-called Red Tower on the city walls in 1490, and in Jacobean and Georgian York brickwork of the highest quality could be found in many of the city streets.

The Red Tower, 1490

at the left-hand side, the product of poor rebuilding after the Civil War

TUDOR AND STUART YORK

The Civil War interrupted this growth and development. York was a royalist centre in the Civil War, and Charles I had his capital here for six months in 1642. The city was besieged, bombarded and captured by the Parliamentarians in 1644. Both Royalists and Parliamentarians in turn constructed earthwork forts for their cannon outside the walled city. All traces of these have now disappeared except at Lamel Hill, on a ridge to the south-east of the city, where the attackers raised a mound to bombard the Walmgate area. The church of St Nicholas was destroyed; other suburban buildings had been set on fire by the defenders to deny their use to the enemy. Yet during and after the siege the city itself escaped major damage, although St Mary's Tower, Bootham, shows clearly its botched rebuilding after being undermined by the attackers. When rebuilding began after the Civil War, fire damage to timber-framed buildings caused the Corporation to decree that new construction work should be in brick.

Late 15th century brick-lined cess-pit

35

Clay pipes for tobacco smoking are common from the 17th century onwards

Remains of a brick town house built in 1690 at The Bedern

GEORGIAN YORK

By the time the royal garrison was withdrawn in 1688, York had entered a long period of civil stability, continuing to flourish as a market town and, decreasingly, as an inland port. It had become an increasingly important coaching centre and a focus for the country's social and professional activities. Earlier street patterns within the walls were altered slightly to allow an expanding flow of traffic, and elegant new walks were built outside the walls. Existing property boundaries were modified and tenements combined to allow for building work on a larger scale, with deeper foundations and more often with cellars. By 1750 Ousegate had been rebuilt and widened, St Helen's churchyard had been removed to improve access to the new Assembly Rooms and Mansion House, Lord Mayor's Walk and New Walk were built, and Micklegate, Lendal, Coney Street, Bootham and St Saviourgate were transformed by the construction of grand town houses. Towards the end of the 18th century we have records of the construction of public buildings including hospitals, the Assize Courts and the Female Prison.

Castlegate House

Late 18th/early 19th century tablewares

LIGHT INDUSTRY

While never a great manufacturing centre, York has been the home of some specialised industries, although the early ones were few and relatively small in scale. In the late 17th century a sugar refinery was briefly in business near the waterfront in Skeldergate, where the partly processed imported sugar could be off-loaded. The archaeological evidence for the industry is the distinctively shaped remains of pottery moulds for sugar-loaves and jars for collecting syrup. Just downstream a glassworks had also opened. In the late 18th century the influx of Huguenots (French Protestants) brought skills in working tortoiseshell, ivory and horn to York with the Rougier family; objects from their workshops have been found in excavations.

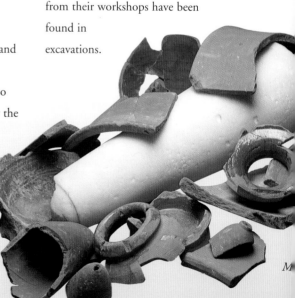

GEORGIAN YORK

Many buildings survive from this relatively recent period, although related archaeological layers lying so close to the modern surface have often been removed in Victorian or modern redevelopment. Archaeological excavation has therefore made rather fewer major discoveries about this era than earlier ones, although there is much that can be learnt about particular aspects of life. The archaeological study of gardens, for example, can reveal details of their layout and management for which there may be no record. At Tower Street the castle ditch lay below a formal garden associated with Castlegate House built by the famous York architect, John Carr, in 1762–3. A 19th century illustration of the house, made when it accommodated the Mount School, shows the garden, but not the elaborate system of drainage below the lawn which employed long shallow trenches filled with rubble. Excavations also revealed the remains of the Georgian summer house, seen in the background of the illustration.

Halifax redware cup from John Carr's house

Remains of the Georgian summer house

18TH CENTURY

Archaeology is especially useful in revealing the otherwise unrecorded ordinary side of life in 18th century York. Almost all sites of this period produce ceramics, including not only the wares that survive as antiques but also humbler domestic vessels. A good example is the group of pots found in a domestic rubbish pit near the Skeldergate town house of the distinguished York architect John Carr. The wares date between 1750 and 1780, when Carr was living in the house, and include fine tablewares such as a Staffordshire salt-glazed stoneware teapot, alongside Yorkshire wares including a Halifax redware cup, and more local coarseware dishes and pancheons from the kitchen. What may have been Carr's riverside garden has also been excavated on Albion Wharf nearby.

...nts for forming a sugar-loaf

Fashion products made and used in 18th century York included horn combs and pipeclay wigcurlers

VICTORIAN YORK

The 19th century was a period of tremendous change and radical alteration for the city of York. The main causes of these changes were, as elsewhere, the rise of new industrial activities, the building of new roads and bridges to ease increasing traffic problems, and the construction of streets of new terraced housing both inside and outside the walls in order to accommodate the rapidly rising population. It is estimated that the population of York in 1630 and later in 1760 was some 12,000. By 1801 it began to rise, steadily at first, to nearly 17,000, by 1821 to 19,000, and then more dramatically. By 1851 the population was nearly 40,000 and by the end of the century it was nearly 70,000.

An important alteration to the fabric of the city was the removal of the outward projecting barbicans of all the major gates, except Walmgate Bar, and the demolition of some of the posterns. New access points were opened through the walls to admit the railway to York's first station in 1839. The first new bridge over the Ouse, Scarborough Bridge, was built for rail and foot traffic in 1845. The removal of the barbican at Bootham Bar and

York seen from Baile Hill, a watercolour by C. Dillon, c.1836

VICTORIAN SLUMS

Archaeological work at The Bedern was not only able to reveal the layout of the medieval College of Vicars Choral, but to show how the buildings were re-used in later times after the college declined. By the mid 19th century The Bedern Hall and adjacent structures, mostly medieval in origin, housed one of the most notorious slums in York known as Snarr's Buildings. Written records indicate that in the 1850s some 300 people, largely Irish immigrants, used two brick-lined cess-pits which excavations showed were dug in the 15th century! Some light on how the residents amused themselves was provided by the find of a chicken leg bone with the spur sawn off. This is evidence of cock-fighting as the bony spur was often replaced with a metal equivalent.

Analysis of the insect remains in an adjacent pit revealed mites, a flea, a cockroach and a number of bed bugs which hint at crowded and insanitary living conditions in what was described in 1851 as a 'modern day black hole of Calcutta'.

15th centu

the demolition of part of the city walls was the first step to restructuring the Mint Yard/St Leonard's Hospital area for the making of St Leonard's Place in 1833–4, followed by a new frontage for the theatre in 1834–5 and the building of the De Grey Rooms in 1841–2. At the same time further changes were made to Castle Yard including the construction of new prison buildings and its massive curtain wall fronting on to Tower Street.

Streets of small terraced houses were built within and outside the walls. Much of the early building was on near-open land formerly the sites of religious houses: in The Bedern, on the site of the Carmelite Friary in Hungate, on the site of Holy Trinity Priory, Micklegate, and at Clementhorpe. There was further development off Walmgate, off Holgate Hill, along Nunnery Lane and outside the walls to the north-east of the city, where most of the new factories had been built. The mid 19th century was, however, dominated by the construction of York's first railway station near Toft Green on the site of the Dominican Friary. The city was fortunate in being home to one of the great railway entrepreneurs, George Hudson

39

The latest (19th century) version of communal latrines adjacent to the Merchant Adventurers' Hall, which date back to at least the 15th century

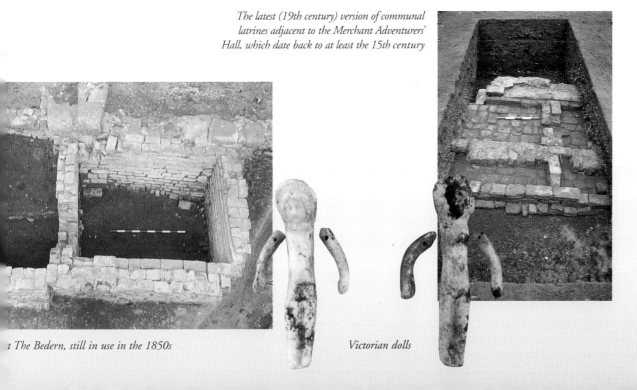

t The Bedern, still in use in the 1850s

Victorian dolls

VICTORIAN YORK

York's first railway station, opened in 1841, lay within the city walls. A detail from Whittock's Bird's Eye View of York

— 'The Railway King'. His efforts revitalised York's economy with improved communications and the establishment of railway workshops.

In the second half of the 19th century extensive works were associated with the construction of a new, larger railway station outside the city walls. Two new bridges were built over the River Ouse in 1863 and 1881. At the northern end of the city, approaches to the Minster were widened by the construction of Duncombe Place (1897) and Exhibition Square (created in 1879 for the art gallery). Railway workers' terraces were built in the Leeman Road area and after the canalisation of the River Foss in the middle of the century there was much housing and industrial construction in the Navigation Road/Layerthorpe area.

Redevelopment continued at a rapid pace around the turn of the century. In the early 20th century extensive housing programmes were begun creating suburbs outside the city walls, as an answer to house a rapidly increasing population and to rehouse tenants of 19th century inner-

40

YORK ARCHAEOLOGICAL TRUST

York Archaeological Trust was created in 1972 in response to the threats posed to the city's archaeological heritage by the redevelopment of the time. Between 1972 and 1997 over 1,000 archaeological investigations have been made in York, including 160 full-scale excavations and nearly 900 observations and recordings during construction or demolition work.

Through its main charitable aim, to educate the public in archaeology, the Trust has introduced over 10 million visitors to archaeology through the Jorvik Viking Centre and 360,000 visitors (mostly schoolchildren) through the Archaeological Resource Centre. The results of all the excavation, research, analysis and interpretation undertaken on the work of the

Trust is available through publications in the series *The Archaeology of York* and *Interim: Archaeology in York*. The archive of records and finds is available to the public and scholars alike. The work of the Trust has benefited significantly through the support and aid of the Friends of York

city streets which had become overcrowded and unfit for habitation. Between the Wars slum areas of Hungate, Walmgate and The Bedern were cleared. Apart from infilling and repair following war damage, little new building went on until the late 1950s and '60s. Demolition and renovation accelerated through the 1970s and '80s in York as elsewhere, providing the opportunities to make the exciting discoveries presented in this booklet.

Mosaic entrance to Ye Old Malt Shovel Inn, Walmgate, c.1880, recorded and preserved by York Archaeological Trust before redevelopment

41

Archaeological Trust, an independent charitable trust. If you would like to learn more about the Trust's activities or become a Friend, contact the Trust's headquarters:
Cromwell House,
13 Ogleforth,
York YO1 7FG.
Tel: (01904) 663000

PLACES TO VISIT

York is a walker's city, to be viewed from the City Walls (open dawn to dusk daily) and explored on foot. Two complementary maps, *Roman and Anglian York* and *Viking and Medieval York* (Ordnance Survey/RCHM/York Archaeological Trust), provide an excellent starting point by placing archaeological discoveries in relation to the modern street plan.

1 **The Yorkshire Museum** in Museum Gardens, between the remains of St Mary's Abbey and the Roman fortress walls, includes archaeological material of all periods from York and its region. For information, telephone 01904 629745.

In 2 **The Foundation**, below York Minster, remains of the Roman fortress headquarters and levels of Roman and later periods found during the excavations of 1967–73 are displayed. For information on opening times, telephone 01904 624426 or 639347. The Minster is open daily; the Foundations and the Crypt have slightly more restricted opening times.

3 **The Roman Bath public house**, St Sampson's Square, viewing of the remains of the heated room of the legionary bath house is possible by permission of the landlord.

4 **The Jorvik Viking Centre**, in Coppergate Walk, includes a recreation of the Viking Age tenements excavated there by York Archaeological Trust, as well as the preserved remains of the 10th century buildings and a selection of the artefacts found in and around them. For information and bookings, telephone 01904 613711.

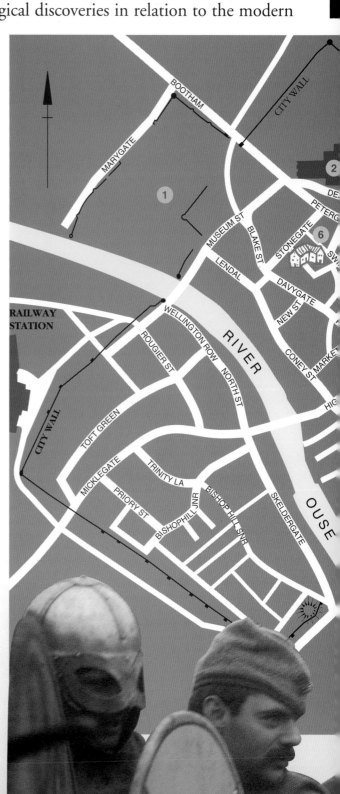

5 **The Merchant Adventurers' Hall**, entered from Fossgate or Piccadilly, gives a marvellous insight into a top grade medieval guild hall. For information and bookings, telephone 01904 654818.

6 **Barley Hall**, Coffee Yard, off Stonegate, is a restored 14th/15th century timber-framed town house. An audio-tour is available and limited events run throughout the year. For details and admission times, telephone the Jorvik Viking Centre bookings office 01904 613711.

7 **Clifford's Tower**, the keep of York Castle, is open daily (closed at lunch time during winter). For information, telephone 01904 646940.

8 **York Castle Museum** contains the Anglian helmet found at Coppergate. There is also a wealth of predominantly 18th–20th century material, including a recreation of a Victorian Street. For information, telephone 01904 653611.

9 **The Archaeological Resource Centre**, housed in the redundant St Saviour's Church in St Saviourgate, shows through its 'hands-on' collections how archaeologists use the objects they find to recreate the past. For information and bookings, telephone 01904 613711.

FURTHER READING

The Archaeology of York, a continuing series, ed. P.V. Addyman, published by the Council for British Archaeology in 20 chronological, topographical and thematic volumes, contains the results of York Archaeological Trust excavations, and other complementary data and discussion. Complete publication list and copies available from Cromwell House, 13 Ogleforth, York, YO1 7FG.

Hall, R.A., 1994. *Viking Age York* (Batsford/English Heritage)

Hall, R.A., 1996. *York* (Batsford/English Heritage)

Jones, M.W. and Kemp, R.L., 1992. *The Time Traveller's Guide to York* (Archaeological Resource Centre/York Archaeological Trust)

Phillips, D., 1985. *Excavations at York Minster 2: The Cathedral of Archbishop Thomas of Bayeux* (HMSO, London)

Phillips, D. and Heywood, B., 1995. *Excavations at York Minster 1: From Roman Fortress to Norman Cathedral* (HMSO, London)

Ordnance Survey Map of *Roman and Anglian York*, 1988

Ordnance Survey Map of *Viking and Medieval York*, 1988

Ottaway, P.J., 1993. *Roman York* (Batsford/English Heritage)

The Royal Commission on Historical Monuments of England, An Inventory of the Historical Monuments in the City of York. 1: *Eboracum, Roman York* (1962), 2: *The Defences* (1972), 3: *South-West of the Ouse* (1972), 4: *Outside the City Walls East of the Ouse* (1975), and 5: *The Central Area* (1981) (HMSO, London)

Wilson, B.M. and Mee, F.P., 1998. *The Medieval Parish Churches of York: The Pictorial Evidence* (York Archaeological Trust)

Wilson, V., 1996. *Rich in all but Money: Life in Hungate 1900–1938* (ARC), 1997. *Humour, Heartache and Hope: Life in Walmgate* (ARC with support of The Scirebröc Group and York Oral History Project)